Jeremiah

POWWOW SUMMER

P●W
SUM

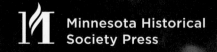
Minnesota Historical
Society Press

photographs by **Cheryl Walsh Bellville**

WOW MER

MARCIE R. RENDON

A FAMILY CELEBRATES THE CIRCLE OF LIFE

To rrr, ssr, and ar—may you always remember that the circle never ends — M. R.

To my mother, who taught me the importance of family. *Kiitos* — C. W. B.

The author and photographer wish to thank the following people for their help in the preparation of this book: the extended Downwind family; Bonita Manzi; the staff and students of the Bug-o-nay-ge-shig School; the Leech Lake Powwow Committee (for the Labor Day and Veterans powwows); and the Red Lake Powwow Committee (for the Fourth of July powwow). The author offers additional thanks to D. & E., J. & L. for helping keep the writing dream alive.

Text ©2013 by Marcie Rendon. Photographs ©2013 by Cheryl Walsh Bellville. All rights reserved. No part of this book may be used or reproduced in any manner whatsoever without written permission except in the case of brief quotations embodied in critical articles and reviews. For information, write to the Minnesota Historical Society Press, 345 Kellogg Blvd. W., St. Paul, MN 55102-1906.

www.mhspress.org

Powwow Summer: A Family Celebrates the Circle of Life was originally published in 1996 by Carolrhoda Books, Inc.

The Minnesota Historical Society Press is a member of the Association of American University Presses.

Manufactured in the United States of America

10 9 8 7 6 5 4 3 2 1

∞ The paper used in this publication meets the minimum requirements of the American National Standard for Information Sciences—Permanence for Printed Library Materials, ANSI Z39.48-1984.

International Standard Book Number ISBN: 978-0-87351-910-6 (paper)

Library of Congress Cataloging-in-Publication Data

Rendon, Marcie R.

Powwow summer : a family celebrates the circle of life / Marcie R. Rendon ; photographs by Cheryl Walsh Bellville.

    pages   cm

Originally published: Minneapolis, MN : Carolrhoda Books, 1996.

ISBN 978-0-87351-910-6 (pbk. : alk. paper)

1. Powwows—Juvenile literature.
2. Ojibwa Indians—Rites and ceremonies—Juvenile literature.
I. Bellville, Cheryl Walsh. II. Title.

E98.P86R45 2013

394'.308997333—dc23

                    2013016072

CAN YOU FIND

THE BEGINNING OF A CIRCLE?

Or the end of a circle? Once a circle is made, it has no beginning or end. It continues on and on. According to Native tradition, the circle of life is endless. It has no beginning. There is no end.

In the original teachings of my people, the Anishinaabe, the spirit of the human being travels from the spirit world to this world at birth. And at death, the spirit travels back to the spirit world. So it is that the human spirit completes a full cycle, or circle, of life.

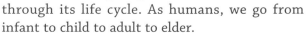

The teaching goes on to say that while the spirit is in human form, it also journeys in many circles while going through its life cycle. As humans, we go from infant to child to adult to elder.

These stages of life can be compared to the four seasons of the natural world. In the spring, tiny leaves appear as buds on trees. Tiny blades of grass pop out of the ground. An infant is like spring, tiny and brand new. As children, you are like summer. Like the plants in the gardens or the trees in the forest, you are growing and becoming the person you will be in adulthood.

The fall, or autumn, of the year is when the food that has been growing all summer will be ready to eat. Gardens will be ready to be harvested. The earth gives her food to the people at this time of year. Adults are like autumn. As mature adults, they provide shelter and food for younger people. It is one of their jobs to look after your well-being.

Finally, winter arrives. This is a time of rest for animals and plants. In the north, snow covers the earth, turning nature white. Some animals, such as rabbits, have fur that turns white in winter. Your grandparents, or other elders you know, probably have white hair also. Because winter is a time of

rest, it is a time for contemplating the past and planning ahead for the future.

In the natural cycle of life, winter is the time of rest and old age. It is also the time of death. Except for evergreens, winter trees have no leaves, and plants do die. However, seeds have fallen to the earth. They are waiting in the dirt for the warmth of the sun and the moisture of spring rains to bring them back to life.

Then, with the arrival of spring, the circle of life continues.

Does your family have a ritual of going to church or synagogue every weekend? Maybe your family has a summer cabin that you go to each weekend. Does someone in your family play a sport, and do the rest of you attend to cheer that person on? Just as your family enjoys these rituals and supports each other in these activities, some Native families go on what is called the powwow trail. They travel to many different cities and

reservations, going from powwow to powwow. Some families go to as many as twelve powwows every summer. The dancing usually starts on Friday evening and lasts until Sunday evening. At the powwow, people sing at the drum, dance in their finest outfits, and visit with friends and relatives.

Many Native families travel to powwows on weekends all summer long.

Since time began, Anishinaabe people have celebrated the circle of life with ceremonies that often included singing and dancing around the drum. These ceremonies were traditionally held with the changing seasons.

In years past, the Anishinaabe held a spring feast in honor of the maple trees. It was the rich maple sap, boiled into syrup and sugar, that gave people energy after a long cold winter. When the sap ran, the people knew that berries and other foods would soon begin to grow.

In the summer, often in June, huge celebrations were held at which people from many tribal nations gathered. It was a time of celebration, as family and old friends met, intertribal games were played, and young adults met other people their age.

After the wild rice was harvested in the fall, another feast was held to say "*miigwech mahnomen*," "thank you for the wild rice." Wild rice was stored for the winter months to be eaten with the deer, moose, and rabbit hunted over the winter. If wild game was scarce during the winter, the people had to survive on wild rice.

In the middle of winter, when snow hung heavy on the pine tree branches, extended families would gather at each other's houses. Families would sit around the fire and tell stories long into the night.

Many Anishinaabe people still harvest wild rice in the traditional way.

Powwows are times for visiting with friends and families as well as for dancing.

It was in this way that the history of the Anishinaabe people was kept alive year after year.

As non-Native people came to our land, some of our customs and traditions changed. Today, Native people gather at powwows to celebrate life by singing and dancing around the drum. Instead of just at the times of the changing seasons, powwows are held all year round. Usually at every powwow, at least one feast is held to say thank you to the Creator. The emcee, the person who tells the drummers when to sing and the dancers when to dance, tells stories and jokes for all the crowd to hear. And just like at the old-time summer celebrations, young people gather at powwows to meet new and old friends. Every weekend, all summer long, there is a powwow someplace, somewhere.

One family that loves going on the powwow trail is the Downwind family. Windy and Sharyl have five children. Shian, the oldest daughter, is twelve. Her sister Ronee is eleven. Sasina is ten, Star is seven, and Bradley, the youngest, is two.

Sharyl and Windy believe that the good that you do for others comes back to you. Remember the teaching that everything is a circle? To celebrate the love they feel for

Sharyl and Windy Downwind with their son Bradley.

each other and for their children, Windy and Sharyl decided to share their family with other children. They do foster care for children whose families are having a hard time taking care of them. What this means is that other children come to live with the Downwind family. Some children stay for a couple of weeks; other children stay much longer. The Downwind family has five foster children. Katie is twelve, Valentina is eleven, Danielle and Keisha are five, and Vincent is two.

In the Indian way, we are taught that adults are aunts, uncles, mothers, and fathers to all children. It is one of the traditions that Windy and Sharyl are passing on to young people in their house by doing foster care.

Four members of the Downwinds' extended family (left to right): Valentina, Danielle, Shian, and Star.

Just as they are all one family, the Downwinds are all one tribe. Everybody living at Windy and Sharyl's home is Anishinaabe. But they are from different reservations. When Indian people ask each other, "Where are you from?" what they are really asking is, "What reservation are your people from?" Red Lake Reservation is Windy's "home" reservation. Although he grew up in the city of Minneapolis, he is enrolled at Red Lake. Have you ever seen your birth certificate? It tells where you were born and who your parents are. Being enrolled in a tribe is similar. A record is kept of who is born to people from each reservation. Red Lake is where Windy's parents grew up and where most of his family still lives. Sharyl is from the Lac Courte

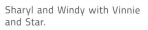

Sharyl and Windy with Vinnie and Star.

Oreilles Reservation in Wisconsin. Windy and Sharyl's children can claim both reservations as home. The foster children are from Turtle Mountain Reservation in North Dakota.

The children in the Downwind family, including the foster children, all attend the Bug-o-nay-ge-shig School on the Leech Lake Reservation in northern Minnesota. Like many all-Native schools, the Bug-o-nay-ge-shig School sponsors a Junior Princess and Junior Brave contest in which a young girl and boy are chosen to represent the school at different powwows throughout the year.

This is a fairly new tradition in Native communities. It honors our young men and women who respect and keep the older traditions alive. Students who are considered for the titles must know the powwow dances, get good grades, and be role

Ronee (left) and her friend Kristi at the Bug-o-nay-ge-shig School.

Shian wearing her Junior Princess sash and crown.

models for other students. At each powwow the Junior Princess and Junior Brave attend, they will act as representatives of their school.

Last year, along with other students, Shian, Katie, Ronee, Star, and Sasina all tried for the role of Junior Princess. Shian was honored with the title. Her sisters felt a little disappointed that they weren't chosen, but they were also proud of their sister and the recognition Shian's title brings to the family.

For the past year, Shian has worn her school's crown and banner at each powwow she has attended. Now, at the first powwow of this spring season, Shian will pass on the crown and banner to the new princess.

Everyone is excited and has been busy getting ready for the big event. During the winter months, Aunt Lora helped Shian with the beadwork for the yoke on her new dance dress, which her mother sewed for her. They also made leggings for Shian to wear over her moccasins.

Shian was eager to learn from her aunt and mother how to do the work necessary to create a beautiful outfit. Years ago, young women would spend the long winter months preparing new clothes for the coming spring. By watching adults create the beadwork and by working side by side with her mother and aunt, Shian is learning the traditions and culture of the Anishinaabe.

Sharyl doing traditional beadwork.

Finally, spring arrives. The Leech Lake Memorial Day powwow is this weekend! Memorial Day celebrations around the United States honor soldiers who fought in wars. Native people

Everyone helps get ready on powwow mornings. Star helps Sharyl make breakfast, and Katie helps Danielle with her hair.

Shian tries on part of the yoke of her new dance dress for her Aunt Lora.

from neighboring states come to Leech Lake Reservation to dance in honor of Native American veterans who also fought in American wars. This is the first outdoor powwow of the spring season that the Downwinds will attend. Many of their friends and relatives will be at this powwow.

Windy and Sharyl will sponsor a giveaway at this powwow on Shian's behalf. They will give gifts to people as a way of saying *miigwech,* thank you, to the Native community that has honored and supported Shian during her reign as princess.

Everybody in the family is excited and nervous. It is warm enough that Windy and Sharyl decide the family should camp out at the powwow grounds. With this many children in the family, everybody has to pitch in to get ready early in the morning. Windy checks on the camping gear and makes sure the van is ready. Star helps Sharyl get breakfast ready for the family.

By mid-morning, Sharyl has lined up the children's dance outfits across chairs in the living room. It is one way to make sure everyone has their moccasins, hair barrettes, and belts.

Shian goes to her Aunt Lora's for one more fitting of her outfit. Last-minute adjustments are made on the other children's outfits. Just when it seems that everything is ready, Sharyl gets a call from her friend Rochelle. She is having a baby! Sharyl has promised to be with her when the baby is born.

After her mom leaves to stay with Rochelle, Shian worries that her mother will not make it to the giveaway that evening. As Shian sits quietly by herself, she thinks about how important

Sharyl checks each child's dance outfit before the Downwinds leave for the Leech Lake powwow.

it is to keep promises. She also remembers that on this spring day, a new baby signals the beginning of a new cycle of life.

Windy loads up the van with the food, tent, extra clothes, and chairs his family will need at the powwow. He also takes the gifts for the giveaway. He counts heads twice before driving off. This trip is short. It only takes twenty minutes for the Downwinds to get to the powwow grounds. Some powwows, like the one in Denver, Colorado, take a whole day to get to from Minnesota!

Vinnie and Valentina help Windy load the family's van.

Dust puffs up around the wheels of the van as Windy turns onto the gravel road that leads to the Leech Lake Reservation powwow grounds. Friends quickly gather to help Windy set up camp in the tent city that surrounds the powwow arena. A canvas tent replaces the wigwams that were used in the past to create a temporary home between the towering jack pines.

Once camp is made, Windy helps Vincent and Bradley into their dance outfits. They can hear the singers at the drums warming up. The good sounds and friendly people make everyone want to dance at the Friday night intertribal dances. When the emcee calls, "Intertribal, everybody dance!" that's exactly what he means. Anybody, from any tribe, can dance during intertribals.

Vinnie has been so excited all day that he is too exhausted to dance and falls asleep as soon as the dancing begins. Bradley steps out with his dad. Shian, dressed in her new outfit, dances every dance and watches anxiously for her mother to appear. Finally, after the supper break, Sharyl arrives with the good news that Rochelle has become the mother of a baby boy.

Sharyl and Windy quickly go over their list as they set out the gifts they have been gathering all winter just for this day. Years ago, the gifts might have been venison, birch bark baskets, or leather pouches. Those were the gifts that were available back then. Today, Sharyl has purchased pillows, blankets, towels, and other gifts to give to honored friends and relatives. Native people are always adapting to the changing times. In earlier times, a family might have given a bear hide as a gift, while today a blanket is a similar gift. Both

Sharyl and Windy go over their list of gifts before the giveaway.

Ronee (second from right) and her friend Awan wait to start dancing.

Windy helps Bradley and Vinnie put on their dance outfits.

Shian greets a guest at the giveaway.

Shian prepares to lead a dance at the giveaway.

are intended to warm the receiver of the gift on a cold winter night. All the gifts the Downwinds have gathered are set out on the ground in the middle of the powwow arena.

With rain threatening to fall, the family gives the gifts to people one at a time. Their friends accept the gifts by shaking hands with Shian and her brothers and sisters before forming a line in the center of the arena. When the Downwinds have handed out all the gifts, one of the drum groups sings an honor song for Shian. This song is a prayer for the person being honored. Everybody stands while the song is being sung.

Midway through the song, Shian proudly leads her friends and family in a dance around the arena. People rush from the sidelines to shake her hand one last time in her reign as Junior Princess. Tonight, as people are dancing, the sky opens and rain falls.

This day has seen the end of Shian's time as Junior Princess. Tomorrow another young woman will wear the crown. This day was also the beginning of new life for Rochelle's son. The spring rain will give life to the seeds that will become plants over the summer months. The cycle of life continues.

Back home, Star daydreams about being princess next year. In her mind, she envisions the new outfit her mom and aunt will make for her. She remembers the man at the powwow with the black-and-yellow paint on his face and the black buffalo on his red-and-yellow shield. Maybe she will dream of a design for Windy to paint on her dance shawl.

She knows this is something that her dad can do because he is an artist. Sometimes during the day, Windy sits outside with the little boys and carves flutes. The boys are too little to carve flutes themselves, but they are learning Native traditions by watching their dad.

Even at powwows, Windy's sons copy his style of dance. As Native people travel and meet other people from other tribes, we too copy each other's style of dress or way of dancing. Sometimes we want to be different, but at other times we may

Windy joins the other grass
dancers.

think that somebody else's way of dancing is more interesting. Windy is Anishinaabe, yet he and many other Native men have adopted the Omaha tribe's grass dance. His grass-dance outfit is made of yarn and ribbons. Windy is a very graceful dancer. As he dances, the yarn on his outfit moves like grass blowing in the wind across the summer prairies.

All around the world, people have special outfits to wear at ceremonies. Easter outfits, prom dresses, and tuxedos are worn for different occasions. At powwows, the Downwind women wear the jingle dress or the fancy-shawl-dance outfit.

Sharyl is a jingle-dress dancer. On her dress are hundreds of metal cones, or jingles. It can take a long time to hand-roll these jingles into the cone shape. To be a jingle-dress dancer requires special patience.

The idea for the jingle dress was dreamt by an Ojibwe man many years ago. This is the story Sharyl tells her daughters:

A long time ago, there was a man who loved his daughter very much. His daughter became very sick, close to death. The father was very worried about her and prayed for her to be well. In a dream, a woman came to him. She showed him how to make the jingles and the dress. In the dream, the father also heard the songs that were to be sung for the women as they danced wearing the jingle dress. In his dream, he saw the women dancing. When he awoke from his dream, he shared his vision with his wife. Together, they worked to make the jingle dress for their daughter. The father taught the songs to the singers of the village. When all this was done and the daughter wore the dress and danced, she became well.

From this girl's family, the jingle dress spread to many other tribes. In the Downwind family, Sasina, Star, and Danielle are jingle-dress dancers. Shian, Katie, Ronee, Valentina, and Keisha are fancy-shawl dancers. The outfit for this dance consists of a knee-length dress, matching leggings, moccasins, and a fancy shawl with fringe or ribbon that floats with the dancer's elegant movements and fancy dance steps. It is

Sharyl and Danielle in their jingle dresses.

Karla, a cousin of the Downwind children, wears a beautiful jingle dress.

Star, Sasina, and Danielle are jingle-dress dancers.

Two dancers in their fancy-shawl outfits.

thought that shawl dancing developed as shawls replaced the blankets and animal robes worn by young women years ago.

The family works on the jingle-dress and fancy-shawl outfits during the week between powwows. Ribbons are replaced, yarn added, and beadwork repaired. Soon it is time for the family to begin packing for the next powwow.

Sharyl again shops for food in large quantities to feed everybody. She is always looking for bargains—on food, clothes, and camping equipment. She is always planning ahead for this big family of hers, and when she sees something on sale, such as material for dance outfits, she will buy it.

While it is hard work for the adults to get ready for powwows, the children eagerly look forward to each weekend. At every

Sharyl shops for food before another weekend powwow.

Katie proudly shows the wind chime her mother, Bonita (sitting between Katie and Danielle), has given her.

powwow, they will see friends from school, make new friends, and get to visit with relatives.

It is hard for all children to be away from their parents. Parents also feel sad when they have to be away from their children. Katie, Valentina, Danielle, and Vincent are very happy when their birth mother, Bonita, attends the powwows with them. When Bonita visits, she tries to bring special gifts for each child.

Bonita also helps the other Downwind children get ready to dance at the next powwow. Later, Bonita and Sharyl will find a quiet moment to talk about Bonita's children. Both mothers share a love for Katie, Valentina, Danielle, and Vincent. By including Bonita and her children in the Downwind family's activities, Windy and Sharyl are creating a loving home for all the children.

There are several different reservations that the members of the Downwind family can call home. But every summer when they attend the Red Lake Fourth of July powwow, they are all Red Lakers, celebrating life within the large circle of Downwind family members. During the day, everyone dances. If it gets too hot, a walk on the Red Lake shore is one way to cool off. Sometimes the older girls help their grandpa at his snow-cone stand.

A smoky campfire in the evening helps keep mosquitoes away. It is also a place where marshmallows are roasted. As the sun sets, the campfire is the only light. Uncles and aunties, nieces and nephews tell family stories and share laughter and tears. Sometimes sleep is hard to come by with all the excitement of the day.

Eventually camp is quiet as everyone rests for the next day of dancing. Windy sits by the campfire to smoke his pipe. In this way, he prays for the well-being of his family and gives thanks for all the good that has come to the Downwind family.

This year, he is also praying for help and strength. A few weeks before the Red Lake powwow, Windy's mother died of complications from diabetes. This is a disease that many Native people live with because we were not used to eating the starchy, sugary foods that non-Native people brought to our land. Windy is also diabetic. But by eating properly and getting enough exercise, Windy is able to control his diabetes so he doesn't get sick from it. Dancing at powwows is one of the ways he gets his exercise. While he doesn't have to

Keisha and Sasina sit around the campfire with their uncle and cousins at the Red Lake Fourth of July powwow.

Windy smokes his pipe by the campfire.

worry so much about his own health, the sadness of losing his mother is still there. Praying helps to ease the sadness.

Gathering at the Red Lake powwow helps the Downwind family in their grieving process. Windy and his brothers cry, pray, and talk together about the best way to honor their mother's leaving for the spirit world. It is customary for Native dancers to quit dancing for a year when a family member dies, but Windy and his brothers decide that their mother would want them to continue dancing.

When their mother was alive, one after the other, the brothers decided to avoid alcohol and other drugs. As they quit using alcohol and drugs, they began dancing at traditional powwows. Their mother was very proud of the choice they made. As a family, Windy and his brothers decide to continue dancing in her honor. This decision helps Windy's children understand that even though traditions should be respected, there are also times when change is good and necessary.

But the sadness is still very heavy. By evening, one of Windy's brothers has hung up his dancing bustle. Today, the sadness is too great for him to continue with the festivities of the powwow.

Windy (right) with his father and one of his brothers.

Dancing is part of the way that Windy follows
Native traditions.

But in the circle of life, the next day is a new beginning. After the tears have dried, there is once again room in the heart for laughter.

This summer on the powwow trail has brought the children closer to each other, their parents, and their extended family. Summer has also been a growing time for the adults. Windy and Sharyl have grown closer as they have faced the death of Windy's mother. They pass on the knowledge they have gained about life, death, parenting, traditions, and love to the children of the family.

In the Anishinaabe way of life, it is important to remember that knowledge comes from many sources. In the Downwind family, the traditional knowledge of the Anishinaabe people is passed down from family member to family member. Adults,

Spending time with the children helps Windy's father honor the circle of life.

who are in the fall season of life, instruct and guide the young children in the family with love and support.

As the leaves begin to turn color, signaling the onset of fall, the family of Sharyl and Windy Downwind travels again to the Leech Lake powwow grounds. At the beginning of each session, dancers wearing traditional outfits line up for Grand Entry.

A naming ceremony at the Downwinds' home. It's important to Windy and Sharyl to teach Anishinaabe traditions to their children.

When the Downwind children hear the announcer say, "Grand Entry, all dancers get ready," they know that as traditional dancers it is time to check their outfits one last time. The girls put on their shawls, adjust the boys' hairpieces, called roaches, and hurry to the arena.

Windy and Sharyl enter the dance arena first with the adult grass dancers and jingle-dress dancers. Sometimes, because Bradley and Vincent are so young, they follow along with Windy instead of entering with the younger boys. The girls enter with the young shawl dancers and jingle-dress dancers.

As each person enters the dance circle, an Elder is there with

Windy and Sharyl, along with some of their children, watch the dancing.

tobacco. The Creator gave Native people tobacco to pray with. As each person enters the dance circle, they take a pinch of tobacco and hold it in the palm of their hands while dancing into the arena.

The children are taught that as they carry the tobacco, the

With Sasina's help, Keisha receives tobacco from an Elder.

Creator listens to their thoughts. So they pray, giving thanks for the beautiful day and thanking the Creator for family and friends. They thank the Creator for the strength in their bodies that helps them dance another day. Keisha, riding in her

wheelchair, gives thanks for being in the center of this circle that celebrates life.

After Grand Entry, the tobacco will be offered to the Creator, either by placing it in a sacred fire burning outside the powwow circle or by placing it on the ground under a tree. As

Bradley goes into the arena with Windy.

Bradley loves
to dance.

Katie and Shian, back in school, talk to Windy.

it is in other cultures throughout the world, fall is a time of thanksgiving for Native people. The food that has grown over the summer is harvested to feed people over the winter. Some families celebrate with a feast, others with a simple tobacco offering. What is important is that thanks is given.

The Leech Lake Labor Day powwow is the last outdoor powwow of the season. At home, the camping gear is packed away until the next season. The Downwind children attend Bug-o-nay-ge-shig School once again.

Winter comes silently and softly in the north. The Downwinds spend evenings reading, watching television, or working on next year's dance outfits. At school, the children learn math, reading, and science. Windy helps Katie and Shian sell raffle tickets for the Drum and Dance Club, which sponsors the Junior Princess contest. It is one of the ways he supports and encourages all of the girls to try again for the Junior Princess title.

Over the winter months, the family talks about the fun they had during the previous summer. They make plans for the upcoming year and for the next summer on the powwow trail. One of the things they plan is a memorial giveaway in honor of Windy's mother. Gifts are bought or made over the winter months. Just as the Downwinds had a giveaway for Shian, they will give gifts to friends and family in honor of Windy's mother.

In this way, the circle of life is honored. In one year's time, Shian was crowned princess and passed on the title with a giveaway. A child was born, and a grandmother died. Laughter and tears. Birth and death. In the circle of a family, in the circle of a community and a tribe, a family is loved and cared for, and grows. The Downwind family returns the gifts given to them by dancing joyously at the powwows, sharing their gifts, family, and love with the larger Native community. In this way, the cycle of life continues for Native people today.

After a busy powwow summer, the Downwinds relax at home together.

The Anishinaabe are most often known as Ojibwe or Chippewa. When Europeans first came to our continent, like anybody learning a foreign language, they often had trouble with pronunciation of new words. Story has it that the Lakota people called the Anishinaabe people *Ojibwe*, which referred to the puckered moccasins that the Anishinaabe wore. When the French came, they reinterpreted the word *Ojibwe* into *Chippewa*. The Anishinaabe people's name for themselves has always been A-ni-shi-na-be, the Original People.

Traditionally, the Anishinaabe never had orphanages or children's shelters. They did not drink alcohol or take drugs. Children were not spanked or physically abused. Children lived in villages with their parents, surrounded by uncles, aunties, and grandparents who cared for them if their parents died. It is this belief in the responsibility of the larger community to care for the young that the Downwind family is practicing when they do foster care.

Windy and Sharyl are no longer married; however, both continue to be deeply devoted to all their children who appear in this book—and who are all grown by now. Shian Downwind, former Bug-o-nay-ge-shig Junior Princess, is married to Waabishkiibines Comanche Fairbanks Sr., and they are raising seven children together. The circle continues.